Easy-to-Read
Folktale Plays
to Teach Conflict Resolution

by **Kathleen M. Hollenbeck**

Hebron-Harman Elementary
7660 Ridge Chapel Road
Hanover, Maryland 21076

SCHOLASTIC
PROFESSIONAL BOOKS

New York • Toronto • London • Auckland • Sydney
Mexico City • New Delhi • Hong Kong • Buenos Aires

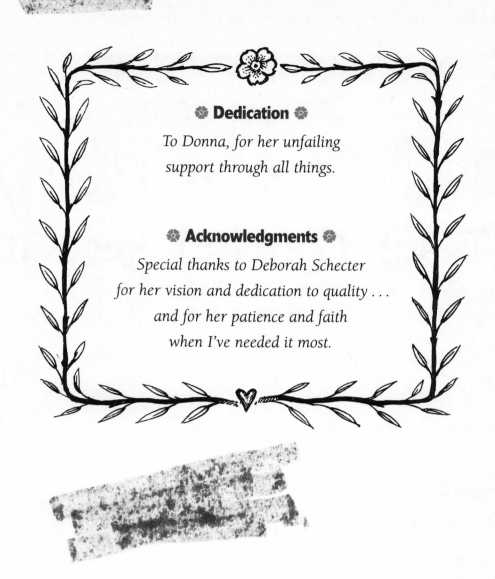

❀ Dedication ❀

*To Donna, for her unfailing
support through all things.*

❀ Acknowledgments ❀

*Special thanks to Deborah Schecter
for her vision and dedication to quality . . .
and for her patience and faith
when I've needed it most.*

Scholastic Inc. grants teachers permission to photocopy the plays and activity pages in this book for classroom use.
No other part of this publication may be reproduced in whole or in part, or stored in a retrieval system, or transmitted in any form
or by any means, electronic, mechanical, photocopying, recording, or otherwise, without written permission of the publisher.
For information regarding permission, write to Scholastic Professional Books, 557 Broadway, New York, NY 10012.

Cover design by Josué Castilleja

Cover and interior art by Delana Bettoli

Interior design by Sydney Wright

ISBN: 0-439-24987-2

Copyright © 2003 by Kathleen M. Hollenbeck

Published by Scholastic Inc.

All rights reserved.

Printed in the U.S.A.

1 2 3 4 5 6 7 8 9 10   40   09 08 07 06 05 04 03 02

Contents

Introduction

$\mathcal{H}$anded down through generations and around the world, folktales reveal the depth of human nature and the substance of a culture. They explore relationships, needs, and emotions and prove that human instincts span borders of race, ethnicity, creed, and location. Folktales serve as examples of human nature at its best and human nature in need of improvement. They act as a valuable tool in the quest for justice, character development, and peace.

The ten plays in this book are based on folktales from around the world. Each play emphasizes one or more ways of preventing or resolving conflict. As you and your students read and perform the plays, take time to explore the message inherent in each one: that peace can be achieved through human behavior and that human behavior, gently guided, can rise to the challenge for peace.

What's Inside This Book

A Teaching Activities section follows each play to highlight and extend the main concepts. Each includes the following:

About the Play: provides information about the origin of the folktale

Vocabulary: previews the pronunciation and meaning of some of the more difficult words students will encounter in the play

Tips for Performing the Play: suggests ways to enhance the performance through props, movement, and preparation

Questions to Ask Before Reading the Play: strengthens pre-reading skills through questions that anticipate the story's main ideas or concepts

Questions to Ask After Reading the Play: guides students in recalling and processing the play's main ideas

Conflict Connection: lists specific conflict resolution and prevention skills that are reinforced in the play and offers suggestions to encourage discussion and exploration of these skills

Extension Activities: provides activities designed to reinforce skills in math, science, language arts, social studies, and conflict resolution

A Brief Overview of Conflict Resolution Theory

In daily life, people routinely encounter conflict. Conflict itself is not bad, but the ways in which we view and respond to it can make the difference between its resulting in peace or in chaos. The study of conflict resolution involves examining skills that we can all learn and practice to increase peaceful communication. These include:

◆ identifying conflicts and recognizing that not all conflicts are bad.

◆ identifying (and avoiding) specific behaviors that escalate conflicts.

◆ learning peaceable ways to solve problems.

◆ identifying, modeling, and practicing strategies for resolving conflict.

◆ recognizing feelings and expressing them constructively.

◆ recognizing and appreciating different points of view in a conflict.

◆ respecting and appreciating differences in others.

Each of these skills is presented in this book. Some are modeled in the plays, some are discussed in the context of how the plays might be altered to include them, and some are reinforced with hands-on activities.

Professional Resources

Hollenbeck, Kathleen M. *Conflict Resolution Activities That Work!* (Scholastic, 2001). Provides teachers with dozens of hands-on activities to reinforce basic skills in conflict resolution.

Kreidler, William J. *Creative Conflict Resolution* (Scott Foresman and Co., 1984). Kreidler provides more than 200 activities designed to help teachers promote peace in the classroom.

Kreidler, William J. *Teaching Conflict Resolution Through Children's Literature* (Scholastic, 1994). The author uses picture books to introduce and reinforce important skills in the study of conflict resolution.

Lantieri, Linda and Janet Patti. *Waging Peace in Our Schools* (Beacon Press, 1996). Presents proven strategies for teaching children to respond to conflict in various situations.

The Frog Prince

Characters

Narrator 1

Narrator 2

Narrator 3

Princess

Frog

King

Royal Cook

Royal Maid

Prince

Heinrich

Narrator 1: Once upon a time, there lived a princess in a castle.

Narrator 2: Near the castle stood a deep well.

Narrator 3: One sunny day, the princess played ball by the well.

Princess: What a beautiful golden ball I have! How high it goes!

Narrator 1: The princess threw her ball very high.

Narrator 2: *KER-SPLASH!* The golden ball fell into the well.

Princess: Oh, no! I've lost my golden ball! What will I do?

Frog: I can help you, Princess.

Princess: How can you help me? You are a small, ugly frog!

Frog: I will get your ball, but you must promise me something.

Princess: *(growing impatient)* Anything. What do you want? Do you want toys? Jewels? You name it. Just get me my ball!

Frog: Promise to be my friend. Let me eat with you at your table. Let me sleep on your big, soft bed.

Narrator 3: The princess took a long look at the frog.

Princess: Okay, I promise.

Narrator 1: *KER-SPLASH!* The frog dove into the well. Moments later, he tossed the ball onto the grass.

Narrator 2: The princess grabbed it and ran toward the palace.

Frog: Wait, Princess! You promised to take me with you!

Narrator 3: The princess raced to the palace and ran inside.

Narrator 1: The frog hopped all the way to the palace.

Frog: *(knocking)* Princess! Princess! Open the door!

Narrator 2: By this time, the princess was eating dinner with the king. She heard the knocking and opened the door.

Frog: *(cheerfully)* Hello, Princess! You forgot about me!

Princess: *(seeing the frog)* Oh, my! Get away from here!

Narrator 3: The princess slammed the door in fear.

King: Who was that? Why are you shaking?

Princess: It was an ugly frog! He got my ball out of the well. I promised I would be his friend. Now he wants to come in.

King: My daughter, you made a promise. Let the frog inside.

Princess: He's ugly and slimy! I can't let him in!

King: You must keep your promise.

Narrator 1:   The princess opened the door, and the frog hopped inside. He hopped right onto the table.

Princess: Get away from my plate!

Frog: You said I could eat from your plate. (*He begins to eat.*)

Royal Cook: (*to the frog*) Would you like your own plate, Sir?

Frog: No, thank you. The princess is sharing hers. She is a kind and true friend. (*The princess frowns.*)

Narrator 2:   After dinner, the frog stretched.

Frog: (*yawning*) This tasty food has made me sleepy. Where is your bed, Princess? I would like to lie down.

Princess: (*gasping*) You will not touch my bed, you slimy frog!

King: Did you promise this frog he could sleep on your bed?

Easy-to-Read Folktale Plays to Teach Conflict Resolution • Scholastic Professional Books

Princess: Yes, but I made a mistake! He will ruin my sheets!

King: That's enough! Do as you have promised.

Narrator 3: Unhappily, the princess led the frog to her room.

Narrator 1: At once, the frog hopped onto her bed.

Royal Maid: *(to the frog)* Would you like another pillow, Sir?

Frog: No, thank you. The princess has plenty to share! She is a kind and true friend.

Princess: *(wailing)* An ugly frog is on my bed! Oh, what am I to do! I never should have promised to be a friend so true!

Narrator 2: Just then, a cloud of smoke filled the air.

Narrator 3: The princess screamed and hid behind a curtain.

Narrator 1: She peeked out and could not believe her eyes.

Princess: *(looking at a prince)* Who are you? Where is the frog?

Prince: I am a prince. I was a frog, but you broke the spell with your kindness.

Princess: *(sadly)* I'm sorry. I was not very kind when you were a frog.

Prince: No, but you did keep your promise. You let me eat from your plate and sleep on your bed. That is the kindest anyone has been to me since I became a frog.

Easy-to-Read Folktale Plays to Teach Conflict Resolution · Scholastic Professional Books

Narrator 1: Just then, they heard someone calling from outside.

Heinrich: Prince! Fair Prince! Your carriage is ready!

Prince: *(leaping up)* That is Heinrich, my good friend! The spell has been broken, and he has found me! Won't you come along?

Princess: I'd like to play with you. You have been good to me.

Prince: Get your golden ball, then, and let's be off! I am free!

Princess: Hurrah, hurrah! You are free! *(They run off to play.)*

THE END

The Frog Prince

❁ Vocabulary ❁

promise
impatient
slimy
ruin
carriage

❁ Tips for ❁
Performing the Play

* Gather simple props to set the scene, such as a rubber ball, a deep plastic tub, a desk and three chairs, and a sleeping mat or cot.

* Give performers a chance to pre-read the play together in a quiet spot. Have each child use a light marker to highlight lines for easy reading.

About the Play

"The Frog Prince" first appeared in a collection of stories published in Germany in 1812 by Jacob and Wilhelm Grimm. Goodness and kindness are rewarded in this tale, emphasizing the importance of keeping a promise and being a true friend.

Questions to Ask Before Reading the Play

❁ What does it mean to keep a promise?

❁ How might you feel if someone did not keep a promise to you? Why?

Questions to Ask After Reading the Play

◆ Why did the princess make a promise she didn't plan to keep?

◆ What did the frog do to get the princess to keep her promise to him?

◆ How did the princess feel when she had to let the frog eat at her table and sleep on her bed? How did she show her feelings?

◆ Did the princess regret the way she acted? When, and why?

Conflict Connection

Use "The Frog Prince" to reinforce these conflict resolution skills:

❁ Keep a promise.   ❁ Treat others with respect.

❁ Use assertive behavior. ❁ Apologize when necessary.

Help children examine ways in which the characters behaved and what might have prompted them to act that way. Brainstorm and act out alternatives. You might say, "Yes, the princess thought the frog was slimy, but she didn't have to speak unkindly to him. What might have been a better way for her to act, despite her feelings?"

Suggestions: Ask the frog to play catch. Bring a picnic lunch to the well. Spend time with the frog outdoors instead of trying to shun him.

Extension Activities

Frog Talk. How did the frog solve his problem? He was assertive (reminding the princess of her promise), but he could have been aggressive (pounding on the door and shouting) or passive (remaining sadly at the well). Discuss these three reactions to conflict. Invite children to give examples of each kind of behavior. Then reinforce the distinction between them with this grab-bag activity. Label two paper lunch bags with the headings "Conflict" and "Behavior." On slips of paper, write various conflicts children might encounter, such as someone failing to return a borrowed toy. Drop these slips into the Conflict bag. Make nine additional slips, randomly labeling them "assertive," "aggressive," and "passive." Drop these into the Behavior bag. Call on volunteers to take a conflict and a behavior from each bag. Have them act out the conflict with a partner, using the assigned behavior. Was the behavior effective? If not, what would be?

Fit for a Frog. Had the princess gotten to know the frog better, she might have found him kind and looked for ways to please him. How might the princess have changed things inside and outside the palace to provide a more suitable place for her guest? Have students work in groups to read about frogs and make suggestions based on the facts they learn. For example, they might suggest building a fountain in the courtyard, complete with lily pads, or asking the palace cook to bake fly brownies or bug casserole for dinner.

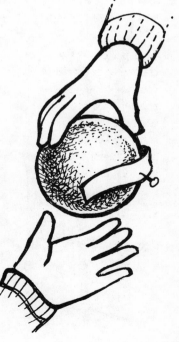

Award the Golden Ball. The princess lost her golden ball in the well, but the frog kindly retrieved it. Circulate a golden ball in your classroom to acknowledge kind and respectful acts. Using gold spray paint, cover a 6- or 8-inch round Styrofoam ball to resemble the princess's toy. When you or a student observes a member of your class being kind or respectful to others, use a push pin to attach a small strip of paper to the ball that describes the kindness in one sentence. For example, it might read "Carlos helped Megan pick up her books." Then place the gold ball on the kind or respectful student's desk. Each time the ball is passed to another student, acknowledge the kind deed aloud.

The Three Wishes

Characters

Narrator 1

Narrator 2

Narrator 3

Old Man

Woodcutter

Wife

Narrator 1: Once there lived a woodcutter and his wife.

Narrator 2: They shared a tiny cottage deep in the woods.

Narrator 3: The young couple did not have much money.

Narrator 1: They were poor, but they were happy together.

Narrator 2: One morning the woodcutter went to work in the forest.

Narrator 3: While he was gone, his wife heard a knock at the door.
(Old Man knocks at the door.)

Narrator 1: She opened the door and saw an old man.

Old Man: I have lost my way in the woods. I have had no food or water for days. Might you have some to share?

Narrator 2: The wife had only a bit of food for herself, but she felt sorry for the old man.

Narrator 3: She gave him most of her meal.

Old Man: *(finishing his meal)* You have been more than kind. To reward you for this, I will grant you three wishes.

Wife: Three wishes! Can I wish for anything?

Old Man: Anything at all. Whatever three wishes you or your husband make will come true.

Narrator 1: The woman could not have been happier.

Wife: What wonderful news! How I wish my husband were here to share it with me!

Easy-to-Read Folktale Plays to Teach Conflict Resolution Scholastic Professional Books

Narrator 2: At once, the woodcutter appeared in the cottage.

Woodcutter: *(confused)* What's happening? Why am I here?

Wife: *(amazed)* I shared my lunch with this man. He granted us three wishes in return! Anything we wish can come true!

Woodcutter: But how did I get here?

Wife: Why, I wished you were here to share the news with me.

Woodcutter: *(growing angry)* What a silly woman you are! Couldn't you have asked for money or power? You have wasted one wish! Oh, that the ears of a donkey might grow on you!

Narrator 3: At that very instant, the second wish came true.

Narrator 1: Long, furry ears began to grow on the wife's head.

Wife: *(touching the ears and screaming)* Eeek! Look what you've done to me! You are a foolish, angry man!

Woodcutter: *(horrified)* What have I done?

Narrator 2: All this time, the old man had been watching.

Old Man: Until this day, you have been poor but happy. Now that you might be rich, you are fighting.

Narrator 3: The woodcutter and his wife looked at each other.

Easy-to-Read Folktale Plays to Teach Conflict Resolution Scholastic Professional Books

Narrator 1:   Great sadness filled their hearts.

Woodcutter: *(sadly)* What a mess we have made of things!

Wife: *(shaking her head)* We don't want riches and power at all.

**Woodcutter
and Wife:**   *(looking sadly at each other)* We just want to be happy together.

Narrator 2:   Right away, the donkey ears disappeared.

Narrator 3:   The woodcutter and his wife hugged each other.

Woodcutter: *(shaking the old man's hand)* Thank you!

Wife: Forgive us for our greed.

Woodcutter: With all the excitement, we forgot what is really important. We have love, and that makes us richer than if we had all the coins in the world.

Old Man: You have shown that you are wise as well as kind. You will be rewarded with great happiness!

Narrator 1:   With those words, the old man disappeared.

Narrator 2:   Months later, his promise came true. The woodcutter's wife gave birth to a son.

Narrator 3:   They stayed in their tiny cottage in the woods.

Narrator 1:   They lived happily together for a long, long time.

THE END

The Three Wishes

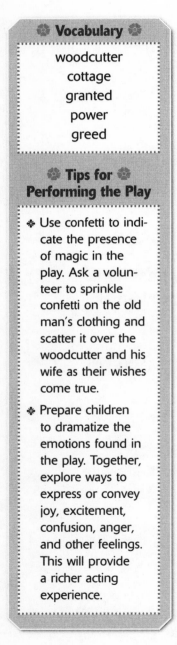

❀ Vocabulary ❀

woodcutter
cottage
granted
power
greed

❀ Tips for ❀ Performing the Play

❀ Use confetti to indicate the presence of magic in the play. Ask a volunteer to sprinkle confetti on the old man's clothing and scatter it over the woodcutter and his wife as their wishes come true.

❀ Prepare children to dramatize the emotions found in the play. Together, explore ways to express or convey joy, excitement, confusion, anger, and other feelings. This will provide a richer acting experience.

About the Play

Several versions of "The Three Wishes" exist. The version presented here originates from the rich folklore of Puerto Rico. A German variation of the tale, in which an elf pops out of a tree trunk, appears among the folklore collected by the Brothers Grimm.

Questions to Ask Before Reading the Play

❀ Have you ever imagined yourself having more of something: more toys, money, friends, family members? What have you imagined?

❀ How do you think your life would change if you had a lot more of any one thing? Do you think you would be happier with the changes? Why do you feel that way?

Questions to Ask After Reading the Play

◆ How did the woodcutter feel when he realized his wife had wished him to the cottage? Why did he feel that way?

◆ What caused the couple to realize they had made a mistake?

◆ Why did the old man reward the woodcutter and his wife?

Conflict Connection

Use "The Three Wishes" to reinforce these conflict resolution skills:

❀ Avoid blaming and verbal assault.   ❀ Think before speaking.

❀ Use I-messages.   ❀ Talk it out.

Ask students to pinpoint specific words and actions in the play that showed characters blaming each other and acting without thinking things through. Write these on the chalkboard. Invite students to suggest alternative ways of responding. For example, instead of shouting, "What a silly woman you are!" the woodcutter might have

said, "I am disappointed that you used the first wish to bring me here. I would have liked it if you had asked for money to help us buy food."

Extension Activities

Poetry E-Motion. The characters in the play experience a range of emotions: happy, empathetic, grateful, excited, confused, angry, afraid, dismayed, sad, relieved, and remorseful. For each word that describes an emotion, ask students to write four words that have similar meanings. Make a simple chart to record their answers. Then have them complete the Feelings Forecast reproducible on page 20.

afraid	frightened, scared, panicked, fearful
empathetic	sympathetic, kind, compassionate, considerate
confused	puzzled, uncertain, unsure, troubled

Create a Consequence Chart. Use a hands-on flowchart to highlight the consequences of words and actions. On sentence strips, write the significant events in the play, such as the old man's request for food and the wife's decision to give him her meal. Tape one sentence strip on the chalkboard. Draw an arrow from it to another sentence strip that tells what happened next. Continue in this manner, tracking the string of events. Then have students consider what might have happened—and how the consequences would have been different—if the wife had responded, "I have no food to share" or the couple had not repented.

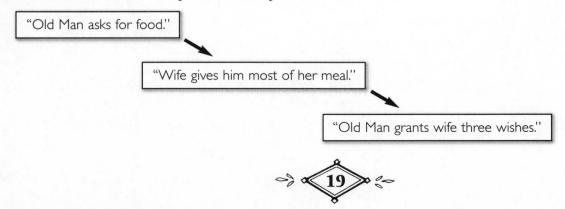

"Old Man asks for food."

"Wife gives him most of her meal."

"Old Man grants wife three wishes."

Feelings Forecast

How do you feel inside when you're angry? When you're afraid or excited? What does your body do? Read the poem below. Write other words that mean the same thing as *happy*. Then choose a feeling and write your own poem about it.

Happy Feelings

How does happy feel to me?
I feel warm inside.
My feet want to jump.
My face wants to smile.
I hum.
I have nothing to hide!

—Kathleen M. Hollenbeck

These are other words that describe happy:

_____   _____

_____   _____

Now choose your own feeling and write a poem about it.

_____ **Feelings**

_____

_____

_____

_____

_____

_____

Write four words that mean the same as the feeling in your poem.

_____   _____

_____   _____

Me-First Millie

Characters

Narrator 1

Narrator 2

Ned

Will

Millie

Ben

Thea

Cleo

Narrator 1: Long ago, in the mountains, there lived a goat named Millie.

Narrator 2: Her brothers called her Me-First Millie, because she always wanted to be first.

(Enter Ned and Will.)

Ned: *(to the audience)* I'm Ned, and this is Will.

Will: *(pointing to Millie, sitting just offstage)* And that's Millie. Me-First Millie.

Ned: Just yesterday, she was at it again.

(Will and Ned look off into the distance, remembering.)

Millie: *(walks on stage, holding a long stick)* Hold this for me again, Will. I'm ready to jump over it!

Will: *(taking the stick reluctantly)* You've been jumping a long time now, Millie. Let Ned have a turn.

Millie: Let me try one more time.

Will: You said that 10 minutes ago.

Millie: Just hold it up for me again. Then Ned can try.

Ned: It's my turn, Millie. Move over and let me jump.

Millie: *(angrily)* Fine. You can jump now. I quit. *(She stomps off.)*

Ned: *(to the audience)* See what I mean?

Will: It's been a problem at lunchtime, too.

Millie: *(pushing Ned and Will out of the way)* I found this stream.
Let me drink first!

Millie: *(elbowing Ned and Will)* I'm hungrier than you! I call this clover.
Get out of my way!

Ned: With friends, it's just as bad.

Millie: Who wants to race?

**Ben and
Thea:**   I do!

Thea: Let's take turns seeing who can run fastest.

Millie: Okay. Me first. *(starts running and singing)*
I'm the best at running races.
I can see it on your faces!
I'm so fast. I run and run!
Watch me go! I'm having fun!

Ben: *(waiting his turn)* Come on back, Millie. Let someone else take a turn.

Thea: I'll go next. Ready, set . . .

Millie: *(running off down the hill)* Sorry, I can't stay to watch you. I've got to get home now.

Thea: Hey! That's not fair! We watched you! You said we'd take turns!

Millie: I already took my turn. See you!

Will: *(to the audience)* Our sister was heading for big trouble.

Ned: Me-First Millie was about to meet her match.

Will: To get home, Millie had to cross Chilly Creek.

Ned: A dead tree trunk lay across the creek. It made a bridge over the water.

Will: Just as Millie came to the bridge, she saw another goat starting to come across. Her name was Cleo.

Millie: *(shouting)* There's only room for one of us. Me first!

Cleo: *(shouting back)* Move out of my way! I'm crossing first!

Millie: You move! I'm coming across.

Will: They both began to run. Neither one wanted to let the other go first.

Ned: You can just imagine what happened next.

Will and Ned: *CRASH!* Those two goats smashed head first into each other at top speed. Millie and Cleo went flying off into the water.

Millie: *(angrily)* Look what you did to me!

Cleo: *(angrily)* What I did? I was there first. I told you to wait.

Millie: I told you to move.

Cleo: I'm all wet now, thanks to you.

Millie: You should have let me go first.

Ned: It was a spring day. That water was mighty cool.

Will: Millie and Cleo sat there and looked at each other.

Millie: *(sadly)* This water is freezing, and we're soaking wet.

Cleo: *(sadly)* Falling that far really scared me.

Millie: We're lucky we didn't get hurt.

Cleo: I didn't think about safety.

Millie: I only thought about being first.

Cleo: Me, too. I'm sorry.

Millie: I'm sorry, too. I guess I learned my lesson.

Cleo: I guess we both did. *(She holds out her hand.)* Friends?

Millie: I haven't been a very good friend to anyone lately.

Cleo: Neither have I. Let's start now. Are we friends?

Millie: *(shaking Cleo's hand)* You bet. Come with me. I've got a race to cheer on!

THE END

Me-First Millie

❀ **Vocabulary** ❀

problem
bridge
reluctantly
soaking
hungrier

❀ **Tips for** ❀
Performing the Play

❀ Place two narrators' seats at the front right-hand side of the stage. This will allow them to talk to the audience without blocking the scene.

❀ Appoint volunteers to review the script and decide what props will be needed. Invite them to create props from art supplies or bring in real items from home.

About the Play

This story emphasizes common courtesy and has been adapted from the fable "The Obstinate Goats," first published in Germany by the Brothers Grimm. The original fable told of two goats traveling down opposite sides of a valley and trying to cross a narrow bridge at the same time.

Questions to Ask Before Reading the Play

❀ What does it mean to cooperate with others?

❀ Why is it important to take turns and share during playtime?

Questions to Ask After Reading the Play

◆ How do you think other children felt when they played with Millie? Why do you think that?

◆ What lesson did Millie and Cleo learn after they crashed? How do you think what they learned will change their lives?

Conflict Connection

Use "Me-First Millie" to reinforce these conflict resolution skills:

❀ Share and take turns.   ❀ Let another go first.

❀ Compromise.   ❀ Work and play cooperatively.

Help students identify the ways in which Millie showed that she cared only for herself: by not letting others take a turn, wanting to be first all the time, and refusing to allow anyone's needs to be met before her own. As a class, focus on the behaviors Millie needs to work on: being kinder to others by sharing, taking turns, and showing that she cares about others' needs and feelings. Let children each choose one behavior and think of a time when they acted in a way that would have served as a positive example to Millie. Have each

student write a letter to Millie, telling her about the incident and how he or she was kind to others.

Extension Activities

Play . . . Cooperatively. Divide the class into groups of three or four. Provide each group with 20 building blocks and instruct them to work together to build a structure that has a specific purpose and displays some sort of pattern when complete. Encourage group members to work together, eliciting cooperation and participation from all.

Good Grammar. Turn positive behaviors into a hands-on grammar lesson. Have students identify parts of speech found in reports of good deeds. First, ask each child to write a sentence that tells about something kind he or she has done recently. Then have students analyze the sentence and identify its parts. For example, what are the subject and predicate in "I shared my snack with Sarah"? In this case *I* would be the *subject* and *shared my snack with Sarah*, the *predicate*. Depending on your students' skill level, you may wish to dissect the sentences further, distinguishing subjects from objects, adding adjectives, and so on.

Write a Rhyme. Reread the rhyme that Millie sang as she ran the race. Have students work independently or in pairs to write their own songs about the benefits of using cooperative behaviors such as sharing, taking turns, letting others go first, and compromising. Display the poems and share them with the class.

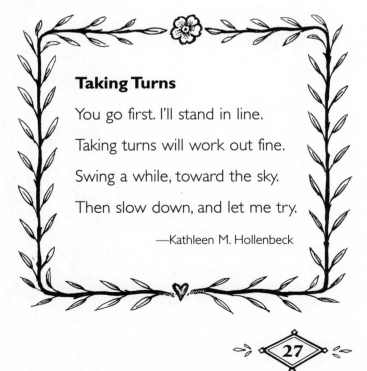

Taking Turns

You go first. I'll stand in line.

Taking turns will work out fine.

Swing a while, toward the sky.

Then slow down, and let me try.

—Kathleen M. Hollenbeck

The Tiger, the Brahman, and the Jackal

Characters

Narrator 1

Narrator 2

Narrator 3

Tiger

Brahman

Tree

Buffalo

Jackal

Narrator 1: Long ago in India, a tiger was caught in a trap.

Narrator 2: The trap was made of sturdy bars. The tiger could not escape.

Narrator 3: The tiger roared angrily and paced inside the cage.

Narrator 1: In time, a poor Brahman walked by.

Tiger: Oh, holy one! Please let me out of this cage!

Brahman: I cannot do that. For if I let you out, you would eat me. That is the way of a tiger.

Tiger: Would I eat one who had been so kind to me? Certainly not! If you free me, I will serve you instead.

Narrator 2: With that, the tiger began to weep and plead.

Narrator 3: The kind Brahman felt sorry for the tiger and let him out of the trap.

Narrator 1: At once the tiger leaped onto the Brahman.

Tiger: How foolish you have been! Now I will eat you up! For I have been in that cage a while, and I am quite hungry.

Brahman: Wait! You cannot eat me! You made a promise, and you must keep it. That is the right thing to do.

Tiger: *(laughing)* I don't care what is right. I am hungry.

Brahman: Let me ask three living things what is right. I will go along with whatever they decide.

Narrator 2: The Brahman walked along and came to a tree.

Brahman: *(to the tree)* A tiger was trapped in a cage. He promised not to harm me if I let him out. I did let him out. Now he wants to eat me. Do you think the tiger is right?

Tree: Is it right that I provide shade for people, and yet they tear off my branches to feed cattle? I feel no sorrow for you.

Narrator 3: Next, the Brahman saw a buffalo.

Brahman: *(to the buffalo)* A tiger was trapped in a cage. He promised not to harm me if I let him out. I did let him out. Now he wants to eat me. Do you think the tiger is right?

Buffalo: Is it right that I work day and night at turning the wheel of a well, and yet people give me spoiled food to eat? I feel no sorrow for you.

Narrator 1: Very sad indeed, the Brahman came to a jackal.

Jackal: Why are you so sad, Mr. Brahman?

Brahman: A tiger was trapped in a cage. He promised not to harm me if I let him out. I did let him out. Now he wants to eat me, and no one will tell him it is wrong.

Jackal: How very confusing! You say the tiger let you out of a cage, and now you want to eat him?

Brahman: No, no. *I* let the tiger out. He wants to eat me.

Jackal: *(shaking his head)* I can't seem to get the story straight! Take me to the place where it happened, so that I might understand.

Narrator 2: The Brahman brought the Jackal to the trap.

Tiger: *(roaring)* You have been gone a long time!

Brahman: Give me a moment, please. I am trying to explain our story to this jackal.

Jackal: He's doing a fine job of telling, but I can't seem to understand it. Now, let's start over.

(to the Brahman) You were in this cage, and the tiger came walking past—

Tiger: *(roaring)* No! No! *He* wasn't in the cage. I was!

Jackal: You were? Oh, my, now I am confused. How did you get in the cage?

Tiger: *(angrily)* Why, through the door, of course!

Jackal: *(pointing)* Through *this* door in *this* cage?

Tiger: Yes! Yes, of course! *This* door in *this* cage!

Jackal: I'm sorry. I am still confused. How exactly could a creature as large as you ever fit through a door of that size?

Tiger: *(leaping impatiently into the cage)* LIKE THIS!

Narrator 3: In a huff, the tiger leaped into the cage.

Tiger: NOW do you understand?

Narrator 1: The jackal quickly shut the door.

Jackal: *(grinning)* I understand perfectly! And if you don't mind, I think we will leave things as they were!

THE END

The Tiger, the Brahman, and the Jackal

Vocabulary

sturdy
paced
Brahman
provide
spoiled

Tips for Performing the Play

❖ Use a large box such as those refrigerators or computers come in to create a life-sized cage for the tiger. Prepare ahead by cutting the box with a razor to make bars.

❖ Have students draw or paint a mural as the backdrop for the play, researching to find terrain and plant life indigenous to India.

About the Play

"The Tiger, the Brahman, and the Jackal" is an Indian folktale. Like most talking beast tales, the story uses specific animals to highlight human character traits. In this case, the tiger represents anger and power while the jackal embodies slyness and cleverness.

Questions to Ask Before Reading the Play

❋ Have you ever faced a problem you did not know how to solve? What did you do?

❋ Why might it be a good idea to ask another person for help when you're having trouble solving a problem?

Questions to Ask After Reading the Play

◆ Why did the Brahman go off to find three living things?

◆ How do you think the Brahman felt after he trusted the jackal? Why?

◆ Might the story have ended differently if the tiger had controlled his emotions when the jackal came? What does that tell you?

Conflict Connection

Use "The Tiger, the Brahman, and the Jackal" to reinforce these conflict resolution skills:

❋ Keep a promise.   ❋ Put the conflict on hold.
❋ Seek help when it's needed.   ❋ Use I-messages.

One of the most important conflict skills displayed in this play is the effort to seek mediation. When the tiger and Brahman could not

resolve their differences, the Brahman sought others' advice. Point this out, and invite students to list reasons that it can be helpful to get others' opinions when two people are having trouble seeing eye to eye. Ask them to think of times when they have asked for help. What happened?

Extension Activities

Sly as a Fox. Animals in folktales often represent human qualities such as loyalty, slyness, and cruelty. Ask students to think of animals that are linked with various traits, such as a slow turtle or a bashful rabbit. List the animals and the traits associated with them. Have students choose one and make a trading card with a caricature of the animal acting in a way that reveals its characteristic. On the back, ask students to write why people might associate the animal with that quality.

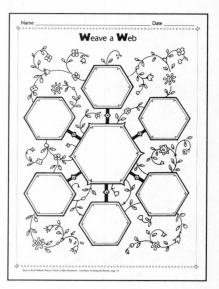

Weave a Web. Make three copies of the reproducible on page 35 for each student. Let them use the page to make a character web for each of the three main characters. Have students draw each character's face at the center of a web and use the surrounding circles to write words that describe that character, such as *bossy*, *clever*, or *meek*. Ask students to circle examples in the play that support each adjective.

Point of View Tri-Fold. Emphasize the idea that different people can see the exact same situation in various ways, which can often lead to conflict. Challenge students to describe a character from three perspectives: as the audience sees the character and his or her actions, as other characters in the play see him or her, and as the character sees him or herself. Have each student fold a sheet of 8½- by 11-inch paper into thirds, as if folding a letter. Holding the page horizontally, have students write one of these headings at the top of each column: Audience, Other Characters in the Play, and The Character. Under each heading, have students write how the person or people named view the character in question.

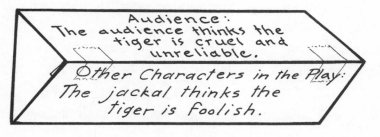

Weave a Web

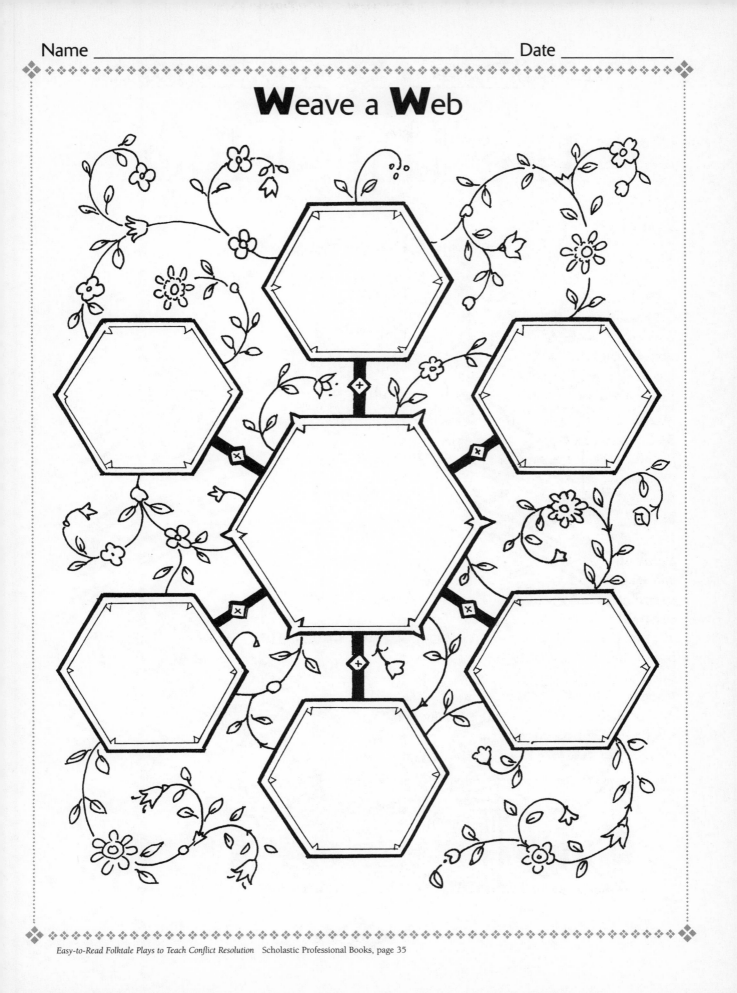

The Half-Chick

Characters

Narrator 1

Narrator 2

Narrator 3

Mother

Medio Pollito

Brother Chick

Stream

Fire

Wind

King's Cook

Narrator 1: On a Spanish farm, a pretty black hen laid 13 eggs.

Narrator 2: Out of the first 12 eggs hatched soft, fluffy chicks.

Narrator 3: Out of the 13th egg hatched a different bird. This one looked as if he were only half-made.

Mother: Why, this chick has only one leg and one wing and one eye! He has half a head and half a beak! He is only a half-chick!

Narrator 1: The mother hen called her youngest Medio Pollito, which is Spanish for half-chick.

Narrator 2: The mother hen loved all of her chicks, but all 13 were not the same.

Narrator 3: The first 12 chicks always listened to their mother and did as she asked. Medio Pollito ignored his mother and pretended he could not hear her.

Medio Pollito: I have only one ear. How could I hear your call?

Narrator 1: The first 12 chicks always stayed near their mother on the family walk. Medio Pollito ran off and hid.

Brother Chick: We spend half our playtime trying to find Medio Pollito and bring him back home!

Narrator 2: One day, Medio Pollito decided to leave for good.

Medio Pollito: Mother, I am tired of this dull farm life. I am going to Madrid to see the King.

Mother:	Madrid! Why that city is far away! You are so small. You might not have the strength to get there!
Medio Pollito:	Well, I don't have the patience to stay here.
Narrator 3:	Leaving his family behind, Medio Pollito set out for the long, slow hop toward Madrid.
Narrator 1:	Along the way, Medio Pollito passed a stream that was choked by weeds.
Stream:	Oh! Medio Pollito! Please help me by clearing away these weeds so I can run freely!
Medio Pollito:	Do you think I have time to waste on you? I'm off to see the King. Help yourself, and don't bother me.

Narrator 2: Medio Pollito hopped on. He came to a fire that was dying out.

Fire: Oh! Medio Pollito! Please help me by putting some sticks and dry leaves on my embers. Then I shall burn brightly again!

Medio Pollito: Help you? I have more important things to do. I'm off to see the King. Find your own sticks.

Narrator 3: Medio Pollito hopped on. He came to a tree. The wind was tangled in its branches.

Wind: Oh! Medio Pollito! Please help me by climbing up here and parting these branches. Then I shall break free!

Medio Pollito: I'm not climbing up any tree. I'm on my way to see the King. Get your own self out, and don't bother me.

Narrator 1: Finally, Medio Pollito reached the King's castle.

Medio Pollito: At last, I shall see the King!

King's Cook: *(leaning out a window and grabbing Medio Pollito)* Indeed you shall! Or at least the King shall see you! Into my soup pot you go!

Narrator 2: The cook dropped Medio Pollito into a pot of water over a fire.

Medio Pollito: Oh! This water feels clammy and wet. If only I had cleared the stream, maybe the water would not wet me so!

Narrator 3: The fire grew hotter and licked at the pot.

Medio Pollito: Oh! I grow hot! If only I had built up that fire I saw, maybe these flames would not heat me so!

Narrator 1: Just when Medio Pollito thought he couldn't bear it any longer, the cook opened the pot and looked inside.

King's Cook: This scrawny chicken is too thin to make a meal!

Narrator 2: The cook threw Medio Pollito out the window, where the wind caught him and whirled him up into the air.

Medio Pollito: Oh! This wind whirls me so fast that I can hardly breathe! If only I had freed the wind, maybe it would let me go!

Narrator 3: The wind carried Medio Pollito high into the air. It finally came to rest on top of the highest barn in town.

Narrator 2: There the wind stuck Medio Pollito to the steeple.

Narrator 3: He stands there today, perched on one leg, with one wing at his side and one eye looking out over the town.

THE END

The Half-Chick

❀ Vocabulary ❀

ignored
Madrid
patience
embers
scrawny
perched

❀ Tips for ❀ Performing the Play

❄ Involve the whole class in making creative costumes and props. Provide feathers, colorful tagboard, craft paper, and other art supplies. Some costume pieces your students might make include a tagboard beak held in place with an elastic band, a choker-style necklace decorated with feathers, and a construction paper kite glued to a tree branch.

About the Play

The selfish and coldhearted meet their fate in this moral tale of Spanish origin. Recorded in the nineteenth century, "The Half-Chick" tells the story of a bird that refuses to stop to help others and learns too late that showing compassion makes a difference.

Questions to Ask Before Reading the Play

❀ What does it mean to treat others as you would like to be treated?

❀ Why is it important to watch how you speak and act toward others?

Questions to Ask After Reading the Play

◆ What words would you use to describe the way Medio Pollito acted toward others?

◆ Did the other characters in the play appreciate the way Medio Pollito behaved? How can you tell?

◆ How might Medio Pollito's life have been different if he had cared more about others?

Conflict Connection

Use "The Half-Chick" to reinforce these conflict resolution skills:

❀ Reach out to others.   ❀ Speak and act with kindness.

❀ Treat others with respect.   ❀ Control your temper.

"The Half-Chick" brings up several critical issues relating to conflict resolution and self-esteem. The conflict in the story—and its unfortunate end—could have been averted had Medio Pollito been kind and compassionate to those in need. Also, while the story may satisfy a need for justice, it also prompts students to consider where anger originates. Sometimes when people act unkindly, it is because they

feel sad or insecure. To deal with these issues:

❋ Talk about ways Medio Pollito might have cared for others and how that might have changed the outcome of the play.

❋ Encourage students to model considerate behaviors that foster a kind and caring environment. Brainstorm and post a list of such behaviors.

❋ Discuss reasons that Medio Pollito might have felt insecure and how others could have helped him build his confidence. Be sure students realize, though, that they are not responsible for someone else's feelings.

Extension Activities

Compassion in Action. Define *compassion*—feeling sympathy for and wanting to help someone who is suffering. Ask students to find examples in magazines or newspapers that show people demonstrating compassion. Have them cut out their articles, staple them to the reproducible, and answer the questions.

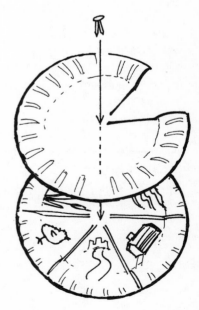

And Then What Happened? On six large, unlined index cards, have students draw six events that took place in the story and write a sentence to describe each one. Working in pairs, one partner then mixes up his or her cards and the other partner puts them back in order to tell the story.

Say It Again. As with many folktales, "The Half-Chick" relies on repetition. Help students speculate about why authors use repetition: to emphasize a point, to aid in storytelling, to invite audience participation, and so on. Then have them make paper plate wheels to record examples of repetition in the play. To make a wheel, have each student draw lines down and across to divide a paper plate into six equal sections or wedges. Instruct them to draw six scenes from the story that show repetition, such as when Medio Pollito tells the stream and then the fire and then the wind that he won't help them. Place another paper plate on top and cut one pie-shaped wedge from it, equal in size to one wedge underneath. Fasten the two plates together with a brass fastener, and have students turn the wheel as they retell the story, exposing one wedge at a time.

Note: To close the activity, invite students to think of other folktales that use repetition, such as "The Three Billy Goats Gruff."

Compassion in Action

Find a magazine or newspaper article that demonstrates compassion.
Staple the article to this page. Then use it to answer the questions.

1 Who needed help?

_____

_____

_____

2 What kind of help did they need?

_____

_____

_____

3 Who helped out?

_____

_____

_____

4 What did they do to help?

_____

_____

_____

5 Did their help make a difference? Why do you think that?

_____

_____

_____

The Ugly Duckling

Characters

Narrator 1

Narrator 2

Mother Duck

Brother Duck

Chicken

Cat

Ugly Duckling

Wild Duck

Swan

Girl

Boy

Narrator 1: At the edge of a farmyard, there was a small pond.

Narrator 2: Beside the pond, a mother duck sat on her eggs.

Narrator 1: *Crack! Crack!* One by one, the eggs began to open.

Narrator 2: Out of each egg stepped a fuzzy yellow chick.

Mother Duck: Five little chicks! How lucky for me! Healthy and soft. Sweet as can be!

Narrator 1: Then the mother duck spied one more egg.

Mother Duck: What a large egg! I've never seen that. It's not like the others. It's rounder, and fat!

Narrator 2: The mother duck sat on the last egg until it hatched.

Narrator 1: *Crack! Crack!* Out came another duck.

Brother Duck: Look at that, Mama!

Narrator 2: The ducks made a fuss.

Brother Duck: That big, ugly bird can't be one of us!

Mother Duck: He does look quite different, but I do not mind. He is your own brother, and you must be kind.

Narrator 1: One day, the mother duck took all six of her ducklings for a swim.

Narrator 2: Each duck jumped into the water with a splash.

Brother Duck: *(to the Ugly Duckling)* You are not a duck. I'll bet you can't swim.

Mother Duck: *(watching the Ugly Duckling in the water)* Nonsense, my duckling. Why, just look at him!

Narrator 1: To everyone's surprise, the Ugly Duckling swam faster than all of his brothers and sisters.

Mother Duck: *Quack!* Little ducklings, come walk now with me. Let's visit the farm. There is so much to see!

Narrator 2: The five ducklings lined up and followed their mother. The Ugly Duckling walked at the end of the line.

Narrator 1: Before long, they came to a chicken coop.

Chicken: *Squawk!* I see five fuzzy chicks round the bend. But what is that creature who walks at the end?

Narrator 2: The Ugly Duckling hung his head. His heart felt sad and heavy.

Narrator 1: Just then, a cat came along.

Cat: *Mee-oww!* What a fright you gave me!
You are the ugliest duck there can be!

Narrator 2:   Feeling sad and ashamed, the Ugly Duckling hid behind a group of weeds.

Narrator 1:   His family walked on without noticing.

Ugly Duckling: I'm not as pretty as they are, I know. I cannot stay with them, but where will I go?

Narrator 1:   The Ugly Duckling set out on his own. By and by he came to a larger pond where wild ducks lived.

Wild Duck: *Quack!* You are ugly. You cannot live here. You'll scare away all of the fishes, I fear.

Narrator 2:   The Ugly Duckling walked on. At the edge of a beautiful garden pond, he found a place to sleep.

Narrator 1:   There he stayed for the rest of the spring, summer, and fall. He hid among the weeds, coming out only at night when no one could see him.

Ugly Duckling: Fall has turned to winter now. The days are cold and gray. I'll hide here till the spring comes, and then I'll swim away.

Narrator 2:   And so, winter passed in this way. As the snow fell and the winds grew bitter cold, the poor, ugly duckling grew more sad and lonely than ever.

Narrator 1:   Then one day, spring arrived. With it came a flock of beautiful swans, swimming in the garden pond.

Ugly Duckling: *(swimming in the water)* Oh, my! I must not let them see. They'll call me names. They'll laugh at me.

Narrator 2:   He was about to swim off when a swan called out.

Swan: *(to the Ugly Duckling)* Wait! Please do not swim away. We'd like to meet you. Won't you stay?

Narrator 1: The Ugly Duckling hung his head. He thought the swans were teasing him.

Narrator 2: As he looked down, the Ugly Duckling opened his eyes. All at once, he saw his reflection in the water.

Ugly Duckling: *(amazed)* What? Who is this bird I see? Is this a *swan*? Can this be *me*?

Narrator 1: The Ugly Duckling raised his wings for the first time. They stretched out wide. They were white and beautiful.

Ugly Duckling: For me, this is a dream come true! I am a swan! I'm pretty, too!

Narrator 2: Just then, two children came down to the water.

Narrator 1: They threw crusts of bread to the swans.

Girl: Look! A new swan by the garden wall!

Boy: He's the most beautiful swan of all.

Ugly Duckling: Such happiness now fills my heart. I feel my life's about to start. I never dreamed it could be so. Such joy I thought I'd never know!

THE END

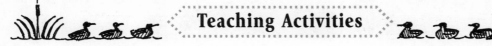

The Ugly Duckling

❀ Vocabulary ❀

healthy
duckling
creature
flock
reflection

❀ Tips for ❀
Performing the Play

❖ Many of the
characters lines are
written in rhyme.
Have students
practice before
performing, so the
verse will flow
smoothly.

About the Play

Loved by generations, this Scandinavian folktale was created by
Hans Christian Andersen in 1844. The story depicts the plight of a
young duck that endures ridicule for his appearance until he becomes
a swan.

Questions to Ask Before Reading the Play

❀ How would you feel if you got a haircut and people told you it
didn't look good? Why would you feel that way?

❀ Do you think it is right for people to say how they feel even
when they know their words will hurt someone else? Why do
you think that?

Questions to Ask After Reading the Play

◆ How did the Ugly Duckling feel about the way he looked? What
happened in the play that helped him decide he was unattractive?

◆ How might the Ugly Duckling's first year have been different if
others had treated him kindly instead of insulting his looks?

Conflict Connection

Use "The Ugly Duckling" to reinforce these conflict resolution skills:

❀ Speak and act with kindness.   ❀ Believe in yourself.

❀ Respect differences in others.   ❀ Show compassion for others.

Emphasize the importance of judging people based on who they are
inside and not on their appearance. Acknowledge the Ugly Duckling's
joy at learning he was a swan, but encourage children to consider that
he might have found ways to feel good about himself even if his
appearance had not changed. As a class, list positive characteristics that
the Ugly Duckling might have found had he looked inside himself.

Extension Activities

Redo a Replay. Rewrite portions of the play—in rhyme—to show the Ugly Duckling rising above ridicule instead of hiding from it. Then fast-forward to the Ugly Duckling as a swan, showing him as compassionate toward others and beautiful—inside and out.

> **Ugly Duckling:** No one wants to look at me,
> Yet I am more than they can see.
> I have feelings I can share.
> I can listen. I can care.

Pantomime the Play. Call on volunteers to reenact the play without words. Explain that pantomime, the art of acting without sound, centers on emotion. Encourage performers to identify the various emotions displayed in the play and to exaggerate them as they act out everything from a chicken's sneering words to the Ugly Duckling's shame.

I Am a Swan. Use the reproducible on page 51 to create self-affirming statements. Have children cut out the swan and its wing. Use a brad to fasten the wing in place so that it covers the three lines. Then move the wing aside and have children use the lines to write three statements that tell something they appreciate or admire about themselves.

I Am a Swan

The Lion and the Mouse

Characters

Narrator 1

Narrator 2

Narrator 3

Lion

Mouse

Narrator 1: Once there lived a great and mighty lion.

Narrator 2: He was the largest, strongest animal in the forest.

Narrator 3: In fact, he was the king of all the animals.

Lion: *(lying down)* The day is hot, and I am weary. I shall lie down here in the shade and rest.

Narrator 1: The lion fell asleep.

Narrator 2: About that time, a tiny mouse came by.

Mouse: These woods look strange to me. I must be lost.

Narrator 3: The mouse hurried this way and that, trying to find his way out of the woods.

Narrator 1: In his haste, he ran right over the lion's nose.

Lion: *(reaching out to grab the mouse)* Who are you to wake a great lion?

Mouse: I am but a tiny mouse, Sir. I meant you no harm. Please do not hurt me.

Lion: *(laughing)* You meant me no harm? You stepped on my nose. Why shouldn't I hurt you?

Mouse: Why, you would just waste energy by eating a tiny thing like me. I am but a snack for one so great as you. I stepped on your nose by mistake. I am trying to find my way home.

Lion: *(thinking)* I am very tired, and I did just eat a big meal. Perhaps eating one mouse would not matter to me.

Lion: *(removing his paw from the mouse)* All right, then. You may go.

Mouse: *(happily)* Oh, thank you! Thank you! I will never forget your kindness. Someday I will repay you!

Lion: *(chuckling as the mouse runs off)* A mouse repay a lion! Fancy that!

Narrator 2: The next day the lion set out to explore a new part of the wood.

Narrator 3: While hunting for food, he stepped into a trap.

Narrator 1: *SNAP!* A branch cracked and a net fell from above.

Narrator 2: The lion became tangled in the net. He could not break free.

Narrator 3: The lion began to roar at the top of his lungs. The sound echoed throughout the forest.

Lion: *Roar! Roar! Roar!*

Narrator 1: On the other side of the woods, the mouse had found his way home.

Narrator 2: He was happily gathering berries with his friends.

Narrator 3: All at once, the mouse heard the lion's cry.

Mouse: That sounds like the lion who spared me! I must go and see what is wrong.

Narrator 1: The mouse raced across the forest to find the lion.

Narrator 2: When he saw the lion tangled in the net, the mouse set to work right away.

Mouse: Don't worry, sir! I can chew through this net. I'll get you out in no time!

(Mouse begins to chew the netting.)

Lion: You are the mouse I let go. Why do you risk coming near me again?

Mouse: *(removing the last of the netting)* I am here because you were kind to me. You set me free, and now I can do the same for you.

Narrator 3:   The lion raised one paw and stretched it toward the little mouse.

Narrator 1:   The mouse was not afraid.

Narrator 2:   He placed his own tiny paw on top of the lion's great one.

Lion: You are little, my friend, but you have a big heart.

Mouse: Large or small, we are all able to be kind.

Narrator 3:   And so the story ends, with the little mouse and the great lion friends forever . . . all because of kindness.

THE END

The Lion and the Mouse

Vocabulary

weary
haste
repay
echoed
spared
risk

Tips for Performing the Play

- Invite students to create a colorful forest mural to serve as the backdrop for the play. If there are woods near your school, take a short nature hike to prepare students for the task. Ask them to sketch ferns, trees, exposed roots, jutting rocks, pinecones, and other features. If hitting the trail isn't feasible, use picture books to set the scene.

About the Play

This story hails from the vast treasury of fables attributed to Aesop. Although nothing has been historically proven, some believe Aesop was a Greek slave lauded for the wisdom he shared with others through brief, moral stories he made up himself.

Questions to Ask Before Reading the Play

- What does it mean when people say, Be kind to your enemies? Why would you want to be kind to someone who is not kind in return?
- Has there ever been a time in your life when you have been kind to someone who was not kind to you? What happened?

Questions to Ask After Reading the Play

- What did the mouse do when the lion threatened to eat him?
- Why did the lion let the mouse go?
- How do you think the lion felt when he realized that the mouse that set him free was the same one he had let go? Why did he feel that way?

Conflict Connection

Use "The Lion and the Mouse" to reinforce these conflict resolution skills:

- Reach out to others.
- Speak and act with kindness.
- Keep a promise.
- Let both sides win.

Help students focus on the actions of the mouse in the play. Invite them to write a letter from the great lion to the tiny mouse, telling what lessons he learned from the mouse that day.

Extension Activities

Coming Soon to a Theater Near You! Have students write and illustrate posters or DVD/videocassette labels to advertise "The Lion and the Mouse." Bring in sample movie advertisements and DVD/video covers to school to show the kinds of details to include: characters, synopsis, rating, reviews, and so on. Display the ads to publicize the play.

What Can You Tell? Have children make observations about the lion or the mouse, based on clues they find in the play (for example, the lion is used to getting what he wants, the mouse is polite). Help students use these to make inferences about the characters that go beyond the play. What is the character's favorite hobby? What types of books, videos, games, or music might the character like? What might the character do if he knew a family member was in danger? How might this character react if someone insulted him?

The Grades Are In. Using their own school report cards as models, have students work in groups to create report cards for the lion and the mouse. Encourage students to grade the characters on various positive traits, such as honesty, kindness, empathy, and wisdom. Ask students to write comments to support each grade choice, and invite them to write about areas that might need improvement.

The Animal Meeting

Characters

Narrator 1

Narrator 2

Narrator 3

Lion

Boar

Tortoise

Narrator 1: Long ago in Africa, three animals held a meeting.

Narrator 2: Each animal was the leader of its group.

Narrator 3: They met to talk about peace.

Lion: Right now, our groups live together happily.

Boar: Yes. We lions, boars, and tortoises get along well.

Tortoise: How can we be sure that we will always get along?

Lion: Let's make a list of rules for how to treat each other.

Boar: First, we must be kind and generous.

Tortoise: We should forgive each other for mistakes.

Lion: We must all share the cool waters of our river and sweet grasses of our fields.

Tortoise: Because we are leaders, others watch what we do. We must live the way we want others to behave. Then we will set an example for them.

Boar: Good idea, my friend! Why don't you tell us how you'd like others to behave? That way we'll be careful not to hurt you.

Tortoise: Well, I am easygoing, as you know. Only one thing bothers me. I don't like to be talked about when I am away.

Boar: I don't mind being talked about, but I don't like it when someone steps on my tail.

Lion: What I can't stand is when someone looks at me without respect.

Narrator 1: The three leaders agreed to remember what they had said at their meeting.

Narrator 2: They would try to be considerate and not hurt each other.

Narrator 3: Then the leader of the tortoises excused himself.

Tortoise: I have to run an errand. Will you excuse me?

Narrator 1: The other animals nodded, and the tortoise left.

Narrator 2: As soon as the tortoise was gone, the lion looked at the boar.

Lion: I wonder what the tortoise thinks we would say about him while he is gone?

Boar: *(laughing)* I have no idea. Maybe he's afraid we'd make fun of the big, clumsy shell he wears on his back.

Lion: Perhaps, or maybe he's afraid we'll poke fun at how slowly he walks.

Narrator 3: Just then, the tortoise came back.

Tortoise: *(angrily)* So slow am I that I had hardly walked past that tree over there before you began talking about me! I knew I couldn't trust a boar—or a lion.

Narrator 1: With those words, the tortoise looked directly at the lion with an angry scowl.

Narrator 2: Seeing disrespect on the tortoise's face, the lion leaped up.

Lion: How dare you look at me that way!

Narrator 3: In his anger, the lion accidentally stepped on the boar's tail.

Boar: *(leaping up, angrily)* Ouch! You stepped on my tail!

Narrator 1: The three animals stood face-to-face, shouting at one another and growing angrier by the minute.

Narrator 2: Just then, a large group of boars, lions, and tortoises came around the corner.

Narrator 3: They saw their leaders fighting.

Narrator 1: What do you think happened next?

THE END

The Animal Meeting

Vocabulary

generous
easygoing
considerate
disrespect
accidently

Tips for Performing the Play

❉ Allow volunteers to pre-read the play before they perform it. You might handle the ending in one of two ways: Either have the performers determine how they will end it, or have the performers stop at the last line and invite audience participation to determine the ending.

About the Play

Handed down through generations, this story had its beginnings in North Africa. It is presented here as a dilemma tale, a story that has no ending but prompts readers—or an audience—to finish the story.

Questions to Ask Before Reading the Play

❉ Think about someone you care a lot about. Now think of one thing that you know really bothers that person. How might knowing what bothers someone help you be a better family member or friend to that person?

❉ If you don't already know what bothers someone you care about, what is one way you can find out? What will you do with that information?

Questions to Ask After Reading the Play

◆ What does it mean to betray someone's trust? Who betrayed trust in the play?

◆ What kind of example did the animal leaders set for the other animals in their groups? Why do you say that?

Conflict Connection

Use "The Animal Meeting" to reinforce these conflict resolution skills:

❉ Avoid blaming and verbal assault.

❉ Talk it out.

❉ Understand and respect other points of view.

❉ Think before speaking

Discuss the idea that the animals in the story talked about being kind to each other, but when it came right down to it, they did not follow through. Each animal allowed emotion to take over and soon forgot all plans for peace. Invite students to reenact the part of the play in

which the conflict begins. What might the lion have said to the boar to redirect the conversation and avoid talking about the turtle behind his back? If that happened anyway, how might the tortoise have conveyed his disappointment in the other animals without hostility?

Extension Activities

Solve the Problem. Help students examine the story from a problem-solving perspective. Using the reproducible on page 65, have them work in small groups to complete the graphic organizer and answer these questions: What is the problem? Who is involved? What does each group want? What are possible solutions? What are the pros and cons of each?

Delve Into Dilemma Tales. Invite students to create dilemma tales from existing folktales and fairy tales—or to create their own folktales without endings. Divide the class into small groups. For those who would like to use preexisting tales, provide children's folktales and fairy tale treasuries for students to browse through and choose a tale to work with. Have each group write out its tale—eliminating the ending—and then read or perform it before the class, inviting audience participation.

Make an Animal-Buddy Bulletin Board. Do animals ever get along in the real world? Some even depend on each other! Invite students to use a combination of experience and research to create a Buddy Bulletin Board for animals that get along in life, such as dolphins and porpoises, or animals that depend on each other in symbiotic relationships (sea anemone and clownfish, ramora and shark, nile crocodile and plover, and so on). Have students work in pairs to research and then illustrate their animal buddies. Invite them to draw, paint, or use collage materials to depict them. Then, on index cards, ask students to write facts about each animal and tell how the two live together peacefully or how they help each other. Display each pair of animal buddies on the bulletin board with the fact-sheet cards.

Name _____

Solve the **P**roblem

What is the problem? _____

Who is involved? _____

What does each group want?

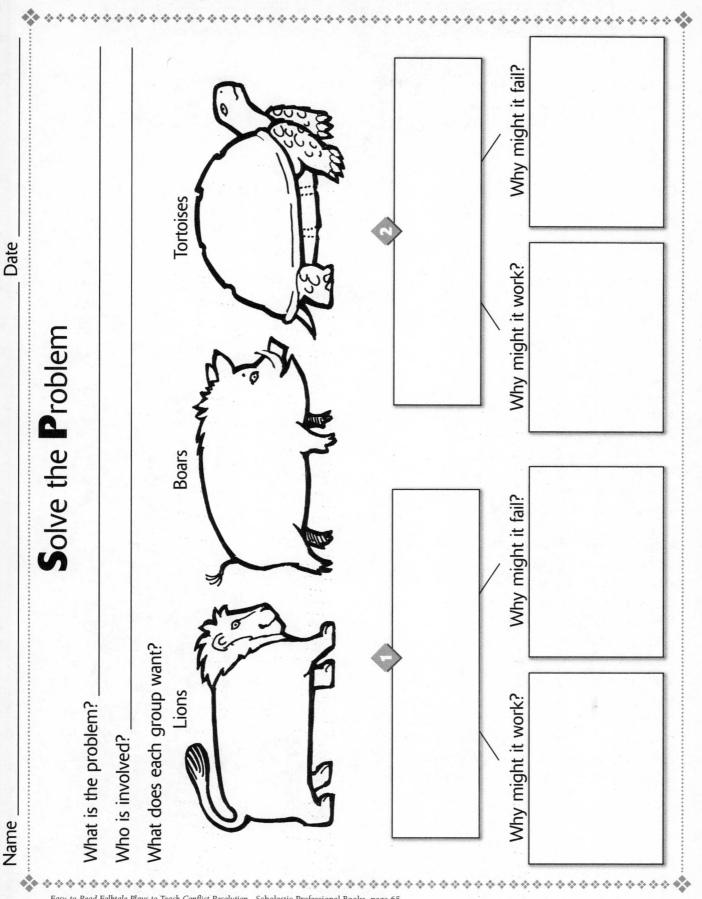

Lions

Boars

Tortoises

2

1

Why might it fail?

Why might it work?

Why might it fail?

Why might it work?

The Old Man and the Statues

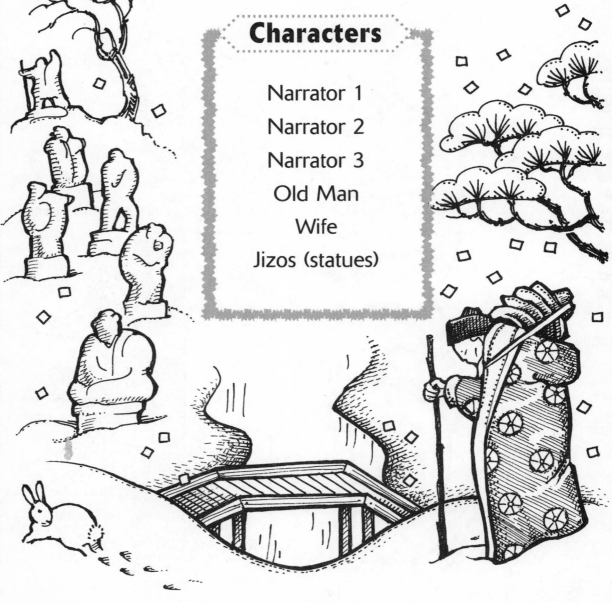

Characters

Narrator 1

Narrator 2

Narrator 3

Old Man

Wife

Jizos (statues)

Narrator 1: Long ago in Japan, there lived an old man and his wife.

Narrator 2: They were very poor. They earned money by weaving and selling hats of straw.

Narrator 3: One day, the man said to his wife:

Old Man: *(sadly)* New Year's Day is two days away, and we have no money at all. How will we buy the traditional rice cakes we need to celebrate properly?

Wife: *(kindly)* We've made five hats. Take them to the village and sell them. Use the money you get to buy rice cakes.

Narrator 1: Tying the hats to his back, the old man set off.

Narrator 2: He walked for hours to reach the village.

Narrator 3: The village was crowded with people buying fish and rice cakes. The man walked among the crowds, crying out:

Old Man: Hats for sale! Braided hats! Hats for sale!

Narrator 1: Patiently, the man called and called for people to buy his hats. No one did.

Narrator 2: At the end of the day, the sky grew dark and a bitter wind blew in. The old man picked up his hats and headed home.

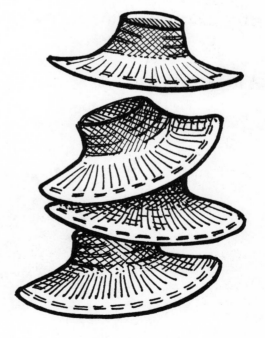

Old Man: *(sadly)* I leave just as I came, without money or food.

Narrator 3: Snow fell heavily as the old man walked home. Cold and tired, he trudged on.

Narrator 1: After a while, he came to a wide open field.

Narrator 2: The old man saw six stone statues, called Jizos, standing in a row. Each one was covered with snow.

Narrator 3: The old man felt sorry for the statues.

Old Man: *(taking off his scarf and dusting the statues)* Oh, you poor Jizos! You must be so cold standing here in this field!

Narrator 1: The old man untied the hats from his back.

Narrator 2: One by one, he placed a hat on each Jizo's head.

Old Man: Perhaps these will warm you.

Narrator 3: When the old man came to the last Jizo, he had no hat left to put on its head.

Old Man: *(taking off his own hat)* Jizo, take my hat, so you may be warm like the others.

Narrator 1: Then the old man walked home through the fields, bareheaded.

Narrator 2: The old man's wife saw him coming and ran to greet him.

Wife: I see you've sold our hats! But where are the rice cakes?

Old Man: *(shaking his head)* I did not sell even one hat. I had no money to buy anything.

Wife: *(concerned)* Then where are the hats?

Old Man: As I walked home, I passed six Jizos standing in the snow. They looked cold, so I gave them the hats we made.

Wife: And your own hat? Where is that?

Old Man: I gave it to the sixth Jizo, so he would be warm, too.

Wife: *(smiling and hugging her husband)* Ah, you are kind and caring. You have made me proud.

Old Man: *(sadly)* Yet we have no rice cakes for New Year's.

Wife: We have each other, and that will be fine.

(The old man and his wife walk into their house, smiling.)

Narrator 3: That night, the old man and his wife cooked the last of their food: some rice and a small bit of sausage. Then, still hungry but happy, they climbed into bed for the night.

Narrator 1: Just before dawn, they awoke to hear noises outside their small home.

Narrator 2: They heard thumping and singing by the front door.

Wife: Do you hear the noise? What can it be?

Narrator 3: The old man and his wife hurried to the door and flung it open.

Narrator 1: There on the step, someone had placed two thick blankets and three baskets overflowing with fish, fruits, and rice.

Narrator 2: On the very top lay two large rice cakes.

Wife: What is this? Someone has left us presents for the New Year!

Old Man: *(pointing into the distance)* Look! It's the Jizos!

Narrator 3: Indeed, the old man was right. In the darkness of the night, the moon shone on six stone statues, laughing and singing and making their way back to the fields.

Jizos: Thanks for the hats, old man! Happy New Year! Happy New Year!

**Old Man
and Wife:** *(calling out)* We are blessed by your kindness, Jizos.
Happy New Year to you! Happy New Year!

THE END

The Old Man and the Statues

❁ Vocabulary ❁

traditional
braided
patiently
trudged
Jizos

❁ Tips for ❁ Performing the Play

❋ Elect a prop committee. Have them read through the play and make a list of props needed, such as hats, a blanket, baskets, and rice cakes.

❋ Children who are acting as statues may want to use face makeup or cornstarch to whiten their faces and arms.

About the Play

Beloved by children in Japan for hundreds of years, this story tells of a gentleman's kindness on New Year's Eve. Despite hunger and poverty, his generosity and compassion emanate warmth on a cold winter night.

Questions to Ask Before Reading the Play

❋ Think of a holiday you really enjoy. What one activity or tradition do you really look forward to every year when you celebrate that holiday?

❋ How would you feel if you suddenly learned that you would not be able to participate in the special activity or tradition? Would it bother you? Why do you say that?

Questions to Ask After Reading the Play

◆ How did the old man feel when he could not sell his hats and earn money to buy rice cakes? Why did he feel that way?

◆ Why was the old man's act of kindness to the Jizos so great?

◆ Why did the Jizos reward the old man for his kindness?

Conflict Connection

Use "The Old Man and the Statues" to reinforce these conflict resolution skills:

❋ Look for ways to meet others' needs.

❋ Speak and act with kindness.

❋ Reach out to others.

❋ Show compassion for others.

Talk about how the old man may have felt on his way home from the village: sad and tired. Here it was, a holiday, and he had nothing to share with his wife. Not only that, but the journey home was long and bitter cold. Emphasize the idea that even in his poverty and sadness, the old man did not focus on himself but thought of ways to help others. Invite your students to talk about times when someone else has done this for them—or better yet, when they have found ways to meet others' needs, even at their own expense.

Extension Activities

Play Jizos in the Field. Play a fun variation of the game Statues. Ask one player to be the old man and another to be his wife. Everyone else can be Jizos. While the old man and his wife leave the room and count to 20, each Jizo finds a place to stand and gets into any position she or he wants. At the count of 20, each Jizo must stand perfectly still. The old man and his wife then come back into the room and approach each statue. The object of the game is for them to make the Jizos laugh, make noise, or move in some way. Once a Jizo is out, he or she joins the old man and his wife in the hunt for moving statues. Jizos can change poses when the old man's back is turned, but if the old man or his wife spy movement, that statue is out. The game ends when one Jizo remains.

Hats Off to Math! Use elements from the play to create word problems for your students to solve. For example, you might say, "Pretend you are the old man and you are selling hats for $5 apiece. By the end of the day, you have earned $45. How many hats have you sold?" You might also provide a list of items the old man might have purchased had he sold the hats, such as blankets, rice cakes, fish, and drinks. Assign a price value to each item. Then suggest a scenario, such as "If you sell five hats for $10 apiece, how much will you earn? What can you buy with that money?"

Write as the Wife. "Ah, you are kind and caring. You have made me proud." The old man's wife used these words to praise her husband for his kindness to the Jizos. Use the words *kind* and *caring* to start a word web of complimentary adjectives. What other words mean the same thing as *kind* and *caring*? What adjectives describe other positive qualities a kind person might possess (for example, *patient, humble, gentle*)? Ask students to choose two words from the web, use them in a sentence, and draw a picture that shows someone displaying

Dinner With the Bears

Characters

Narrator 1

Narrator 2

Narrator 3

Hunter

Wind

Grizzly Bears

Largest Bear

Villager 1

Villager 2

Narrator 1:   Long ago, there lived a hunter who was very old.

Narrator 2:   His wife and all of his friends had long since died. The hunter was very lonely.

Narrator 3:   One day the hunter said to himself:

Hunter: I have hunted and killed many bears in my lifetime. It is right that the bears should feast on me.

Narrator 1:   So the hunter closed his cabin and left his belongings behind.

Narrator 2:   He walked to a river filled with salmon and sat on a rock to wait.

Narrator 3:   While the hunter waited, the wind spoke to him.

Wind: Old man, why do you sit by the water?

Hunter: I am waiting for the bears. They will come here to find fish for their supper. Instead, they will find me.

Narrator 1:   Just then, the hunter heard twigs snapping in the woods nearby.

Narrator 2:   He looked up to see three enormous grizzly bears stepping out of the forest.

(The Grizzly Bears enter.)

Narrator 3:   All at once, the hunter grew frightened. As the largest of the bears came toward him, the hunter jumped up.

Hunter: Wait! Don't eat me! I have come to invite you to a feast!

Largest Bear: *(growling angrily)* GRRR! GRRR!

Hunter: I am old, and I have no family or friends. Please come to my home tomorrow afternoon. I will serve you a feast fit for kings.

Narrator 1:   The largest bear whined at the other bears. All at once, the three turned away from the hunter. They headed back into the woods.

Hunter: *(to the wind)* Imagine that! I was to be dinner for the bears and now I am making dinner for them!

Wind: Hurry along, old man. You have food to prepare!

Narrator 2:   The hunter raced back to his cabin. He spent all that night and the next morning preparing for the feast.

Narrator 1:   He swept his cabin, washed dishes, and set the table. He fished and gathered berries.

Narrator 2:   People in the village came to see what was going on.

Villager 1:   You have enough food here to feed our whole village! What are you doing?

Hunter: I have invited three grizzly bears to feast in my home.

Villager 2:   You've invited grizzly bears to your table? You have lost your senses!

Villager 1: You will be the feast, not these berries and fish!

Hunter: We shall see. We shall see.

Narrator 3: By noontime, the hunter was ready. He painted red stripes on his arms and chest to celebrate the feast.

Narrator 1: The bears walked out of the forest and through the village. Villagers screamed and ran into their homes.

Narrator 2: The hunter, however, stood in his doorway. Arms wide, he welcomed the bears.

Hunter: Welcome, my friends! Sit here in my home and feast with me.

Grizzly Bears: *Grrr! Grrr!*

Narrator 3: The three bears sat at the hunter's table.

Narrator 1: They feasted on baskets of strawberries, blueberries, and salmon. The hunter told stories of his adventures in the forest, and the bears shared stories, too.

Grizzly Bears: (*moving paws to tell a story*) *Grrr! Grrr!*

Narrator 2: At last, the feast ended and the hunter bid his new friends good-bye. As they left the cabin, the bears in turn licked off the hunter's red paint.

Hunter: It is as if you are licking away my sorrow. Good-bye, my friends!

Narrator 3: That night, the hunter dreamed that the largest of the bears spoke to him in his own language.

Largest Bear: Thank you for your kindness, old man. Like you, I have lived a long time and have lost those I love. I, too, have felt lonely and sad. Please consider me your friend. When you feel sad, think of me. You are not alone anymore.

Narrator 1: As the dream ended, a cool wind blew through the cabin.

Wind: Today you treated beasts with kindness. In your wisdom, you have turned enemies into friends.

THE END

Dinner With the Bears

❀ Vocabulary ❀

belongings
salmon
whined
adventures
language
wisdom

❀ Tips for Performing the Play

❖ Select several students to work together to create sound-effects for the performance. They might pour water into a basin to emulate the river, snap twigs as the bears approach, and play music to indicate the hunter's changing feelings of sadness, fear, and peace.

❖ Invite the audience to participate with their voices. Have them scream on cue as villagers react to the bears walking through their town.

About the Play

"Dinner With the Bears" is based on a myth handed down by the Tlingit peoples of Alaska. Originally titled "The Man Who Entertained the Bears," it first appeared in the 1909 edition of *Tlingit Myths and Texts*.

Questions to Ask Before Reading the Play

❀ What kinds of things do people do to show kindness to others?

❀ How might being kind to someone else affect the way they act?

Questions to Ask After Reading the Play

❀ Why did the man wait by the river for the bears to come?

❀ Why did the man invite the bears to dinner?

❀ How did the man's kindness affect the bears? How do you know this?

Conflict Connection

Use "Dinner With the Bears" to reinforce these conflict resolution skills:

❀ Let both sides win.   ❀ Look for ways to meet others' needs.

❀ Be an active listener.   ❀ Treats others with kindness.

Talk with students about what it means to find a "win-win" solution to a problem (solving the problem in a way that meets the needs of everyone involved). Help students identify the win-win solution in the play: The hunter invited the bears to dinner and befriended them, ensuring his own safety by giving the bears food to satisfy their hunger. Talk about other alternatives that might have provided a win-win solution. For example, the hunter might have offered to collect fish for the bears right then, providing them with food in exchange for his life.

Extension Activities

Listen Up! Although it must have been difficult to communicate with bears, the hunter managed to form a friendship that night. Surely, good listening skills played a part. As a class, list things good listeners do to show that they are hearing and understanding the speaker, such as focusing attention on the speaker, nodding or responding briefly to show understanding, trying not to interrupt, and repeating in similar words what the speaker has said. Have students then role play the hunter and his guests, modeling some of the listening skills they might have used with one another at dinner.

Just the Bear Facts. Use the reproducible activity on page 80 to help students interview the bears. Divide the class into pairs. Ask one person in each pair to be an interviewer and the other, a bear from the story. Students can write their answers directly on the reproducible page. You may want to have partners reverse roles and conduct a second interview.

Dinner . . . or Danger? Fortunately for the hunter, his quick thinking led to a peaceful solution. How might the story have been different if the hunter had not decided to befriend his enemies? What might have happened instead? Invite students to draw story strips that show alternate scenarios. Have them begin with the scene in which the hunter first sees the bears. To make the story strips, give each student a strip of paper (8½ by 11 inches, cut in half lengthwise). Instruct students to hold the strip horizontally and fold it in half, then in half again, to make four equal sections for drawing.

Name _____ Date _____

Just the Bear Facts

◇ What is your name? _____
◇ Where do you live? _____
◇ What are your favorite foods? _____

◇ Describe what happened when you first met the hunter at the river.
_____

◇ How did you feel when the hunter asked you to dinner? Why did you feel that way? _____

◇ How did you feel as you walked through the village? Why?
_____

◇ What did it feel like to be inside the hunter's house?
_____

◇ What did you talk about at the table? _____

◇ What did you like most about the evening you spent at the hunter's?
_____

Just the Bear Facts

1 What is your name? _____

2 Where do you live? _____

3 What are your favorite foods? _____

_____

_____

4 Describe what happened when you first met the hunter at the river.

_____

_____

5 How did you feel when the hunter asked you to dinner? Why did you

feel that way? _____

_____

_____

6 How did you feel as you walked through the village? Why?

_____

_____

7 What did it feel like to be inside the hunter's house?

_____

_____

8 What did you talk about at the table? _____

_____

_____

9 What did you like most about the evening you spent at the hunter's?

_____

_____